Live a Simple Life

THE INFLUENCER BOOK

ANTONIO P. SERRANO M.D.

Balboa Press books may be ordered through booksellers or by contacting:

Balboa Press
A Division of Hay House
1663 Liberty Drive
Bloomington, IN 47403
www.balboapress.com
1 (877) 407-4847

Because of the dynamic nature of the Internet, any web addresses or links contained in this book may have changed since publication and may no longer be valid. The views expressed in this work are solely those of the author and do not necessarily reflect the views of the publisher, and the publisher hereby disclaims any responsibility for them.

Any people depicted in stock imagery provided by Getty Images are models, and such images are being used for illustrative purposes only. Certain stock imagery © Getty Images.

ISBN: 978-1-9822-1794-5 (sc)
978-1-9822-1793-8 (e)

Print information available on the last page.

Library of Congress Control Number: 2018914598

Balboa Press rev. date: 12/19/2018

BALBOA
PRESS
A DIVISION OF HAY HOUSE

"The only source of knowledge is experience"

By Albert Einstein

Divide your life into 3 chapters:
1. *30 years of study and/or education.*
2. *30 years of making money*
3. *30 years of retirement and sharing words of wisdom, material and non-material things.*

By Andrew Carnegie

Make your personal decisions depending on these four factors:
1. *Humility*
2. *Gratitude*
3. *Simplicity*
4. *Mindfulness*

By Antonio P. Serrano, MD

TABLE OF CONTENTS

Foreword.. vii

Preface.. viii

Dedication 1

English Version 4

Spanish Version 5

Chinese Version... 6

German Version 7

Russian Version 8

French Version 9

Etiquette 12

Limit Your Association With These People. 14

What Is The Dash Diet 15

Ideal Weight.. 16

Vital Signs... 19

Blood Sugar Levels 21

Modern Medicine Cabinet 22

Recommended Links For Everybody: 23

References 24

Important Telephone Numbers 25

This site or book is not intended to provide and does not constitute medical, health, legal, financial or other professional advice.

DISCLAIMER

FOREWORD

I am Ana Hernandez, Dr Serrano's' technical advisor. I have been working with Dr Serrano in this book. I've come to realization this book could inspire a lot of people, mainly for children, grandchildren and new generation. Dr Serrano is not only a great doctor but also a great inspiration. I've enjoyed working on this book with him not only because it's an awesome book but also because it has helped me Live A Simple Life.

Our dad has been a great influence in our lives. He has encouraged us to have a dream and strive for that dream. The importance of providing for our families, having good moral standing and being a law abiding citizen. He wasn't home much because he was seeing patients in the hospital, so we valued the time when he was free and spent time with us. We would go to the medical clinic and stayed in his office and make rounds in the hospital with him.

He is dedicating this book to his 7 grandkids: Ashton, Hayleigh, Ayden, Ella, Lily, Mia, and Cordelia.

SIGNED BY: KENN, JUSTIN, AND CHRIS.

PREFACE

I am Antonio P Serrano, M.D, I have been a General Practitioner in Arlington TX for 20 years. Live A Simple Life was initially written to my grandchildren. I believe the lessons I have learned from Life would guide my grandchildren in their Life's Journey.

As I was writing the book I have realized that I could spread and share the message in the book. I thought the message would help to create a civilized new generation and responsible citizens.

I DEDICATE THIS BOOK TO MY GRANDCHILDREN,

ASHTON

HAYLEIGH

AYDEN

ELLA

LILY

MIA

CORDELIA

Edit

Tony Serrano

Antonio P. Serrano, M.D. Author of Live A Simple Life. Founder of InstantTravel and DocsNow.global

"Live a simple life" by Antonio P. Serrano, MD. I have learned through the years the following and has guided me through life: Live in the moment; love your job and be proud of your work; have internal strength; surround yourself with dreamers and positive people; be self-reliant and be resourceful; get 7-8 hour nightly sleep; have a nutritious DASH or Mediterranean diet and maintain an ideal weight; have a daily 30 minute walk or exercise; avoid alcoholic drinks, never smoke and never use illegal addictive drugs ; have an enjoyable day and a spiritual weekend; as much as possible have your iPhone or android phone with you, learn self-defense and avoid dangerous situation and places; drive within the speed limit; make sure your car is safe and dependable; take your daily supplements, vitamins and prescription medicines; learn CPR and First Aid; have positive mental happy attitude; keep your place clean and organized and wash your dishes every night; recycle used plastics and papers; learn cooking; learn to play a musical instrument; have a hobby or participate in sport; learn a foreign language; take good care of a pet; read stories about successful men and women; read good inspirational book everyday; practice what is ethical; know your legal rights; sometimes it is better to be happy than right; know your personal space and personal boundaries; be prepared for anything that life throws at you and do your homework; maintain a strong family and community ties; avoid arguments about religion, politics and money; volunteer for charitable causes; donate used clothes to charity; stay responsible and true to yourself; contribute some time and financial help to charity and church; travel to your favorite places; enjoy a good show; keep up with current events; have an education, skills or talents; continue to learn something new everyday; learn beautiful places from InstantTravelLinks.com and see the world; read and review some high school and college subjects from KhanAcademy.org; entertain yourself by watching and learning from YouTube.com; keep up with technology; when in doubt google it or get a second opinion; do everything legal; keep in touch with relatives; former friends and classmates; stay courageous in the face of adversities, having faith you will withstand the "storm" or difficulties of life, do not lose hope, stay composed, face the problem head on and accept the consequences of your situation, and with the passage of time things will get better; keep good relationship and stay away from toxic relationship and dysfunctional living; learn and understand the 12-step meeting; own your fault and acknowledge your mistake; say you are sorry and mean it; do not be too proud to ask for help; count your blessing everyday; take care of your monthly financial responsibilities; have savings, emergency funds good for at least a year, have investments and have a nest egg for your retirement; have a life and disability insurance: pay your taxes on time; celebrate special events; have a regular dental and medical check-up; have a regular doctor, a dentist, an accountant and a lawyer; keep records of important events; be sure to pray and meditate every night; make a monthly lists of things that you are thankful for and have daily gratitude attitude; be respectful and kind to others; be mindful of others; be tolerant of people different from you; be kind, humble, generous and share your wisdom and professional knowledge with your family; never dishonor your family and be the best role model to your children. Share these words of wisdom with family or friends or somebody you love and care. I wish you a blessed, happy, healthy, peaceful and a successful life.

Vive una vida sencilla" por Antonio P. Serrano, MD. He aprendido a través de los años y me has guiado a través de la vida: vive en el momento, ama tu trabajo y siéntete orgulloso de tu trabajo, ten fuerza interna, rodéate con soñadores y personas positivas, ser autosuficiente y tener recursos, dormir de 7 a 8 horas todas las noches, tener una dieta DASH o mediterránea nutritiva y mantener un peso ideal, hacer caminatas diarias de 30 minutos o hacer ejercicio, evitar las bebidas alcohólicas, nunca fumar y nunca use drogas adictivas ilegales, tenga un día agradable y un fin de semana espiritual; en la medida de lo posible lleve consigo su iPhone o teléfono Android, aprenda defensa personal y evite lugares y situaciones peligrosas, maneje dentro del límite de velocidad, asegúrese de que su automóvil sea seguro y confiable, tome sus suplementos diarios, vitaminas y medicamentos recetados, aprenda RCP y primeros auxilios, tenga una actitud feliz y positiva mental, mantenga su lugar limpio y organizado y lave sus platos todas las noches, recicle plásticos y papeles usados; aprende a cocinar; aprende a tocar un instrumento musical; tener un hobby o participar en el deporte; aprenda un idioma extranjero; cuida bien a una mascota; leer historias sobre hombres y mujeres exitosos; leer un buen libro de inspiración todos los días; practica lo que es ético; conocer sus derechos legales; a veces es mejor ser feliz que correcto; conoce tu espacio personal y tus límites personales; prepárate para cualquier cosa que la vida te depare y haz tu tarea; mantener fuertes lazos familiares y comunitarios; evitar discusiones sobre religión, política y dinero; se voluntario para causas caritativas; donar ropa usada a la caridad; mantente responsable y fiel a ti mismo; contribuir un poco de tiempo y ayuda financiera a la caridad y la iglesia; viaja a tus lugares favoritos; disfruta de un buen espectáculo; mantenerse al día con los eventos actuales; tener una educación, habilidades o talentos; continuar aprendiendo algo nuevo todos los días; aprende hermosos lugares de InstantTravelLinks.com y conoce el mundo; leer y revisar algunas materias de la escuela secundaria y la universidad de KhanAcademy.org; entretenerse mirando y aprendiendo de YouTube.com; mantente al día con la tecnología como la Impresora en 3D; Robotica; Nano Tecnologia ; Terapia de Stem Cell; Ingeniera Genetica; e Intelegencia Artificial; en caso de duda google o obtener una segunda opinión; hacer todo legal; mantente valiente frente a las adversidades, teniendo fe resistirás la "tormenta" o las dificultades de la vida, no pierdas la esperanza, mantén la compostura, enfrenta el problema de frente y acepta las consecuencias de tu situación, y con el paso del tiempo las cosas estara mejor; mantenerse en contacto con parientes; amigos antiguos y compañeros de clase; mantener una buena relación y evitar las relaciones tóxicas y la vida disfuncional; aprende y entiende la reunión de 12 pasos; posee tu culpa y reconoce tu error; di que lo sientes y lo dices en serio; no seas demasiado orgulloso para pedir ayuda; cuenta tu bendición todos los días; cuide sus responsabilidades financieras mensuales; tener ahorros, fondos de emergencia que sean buenos durante al menos un año, tener inversiones y tener un huevo para su jubilación; tener un seguro de vida e incapacidad: pagar sus impuestos a tiempo; celebrar eventos especiales; tener un chequeo dental y médico regular; tener un médico regular, un dentista, un contador y un abogado; mantener registros de eventos importantes; asegúrese de orar y meditar todas las noches; haga una lista mensual de las cosas por las que está agradecido y tenga una actitud de gratitud diaria; ser respetuoso y amable con los demás; ser consciente de los demás; ser tolerante con las personas diferentes de ti; sea amable, humilde, generoso y comparta su sabiduría y conocimiento profesional con su familia; nunca deshonre a su familia y sea el mejor modelo para sus hijos. Comparte estas palabras de sabiduría con familiares o amigos o con alguien a quien ames y te importe. Te deseo una vida bendecida, feliz, saludable, pacífica y exitosa.

"Live a simple life " by Antonio P. Serrano, MD. I have learned through the years the following and has guided me through life: Live in the moment; love your job and be proud of your work; have internal strength; surround yourself with dreamers and positive people; be self-reliant and be resourceful; get 7-8 hour nightly sleep; have a nutritious DASH or Mediterranean diet and maintain an ideal weight; have a daily 30 minute walk or exercise; avoid alcoholic drinks, never smoke and never use illegal addictive drugs ; have an enjoyable day and a spiritual weekend; as much as possible have your iPhone or android phone with you, learn self-defense and avoid dangerous situation and places; drive within the speed limit; make sure your car is safe and dependable; take your daily supplements, vitamins and prescription medicines; learn CPR and First Aid; have positive mental happy attitude; keep your place clean and organized and wash your dishes every night; recycle used plastics and papers; learn cooking; learn to play a musical instrument; have a hobby or participate in sport; learn a foreign language; take good care of a pet; read stories about successful men and women; read good inspirational book every day; practice what is ethical; know your legal rights; sometimes it is better to be happy than right; know your personal space and personal boundaries; be prepared for anything that life throws at you and do your homework; maintain a strong family and community ties; avoid arguments about religion, politics and money; volunteer for charitable causes; donate used clothes to charity; stay responsible and true to yourself; contribute some time and financial help to charity and church; travel to your favorite places; enjoy a good show; keep up with current events; have an education, skills or talents; continue to learn something new every day; learn beautiful places from InstantTravelLinks. com and see the world; read and review some high school and college subjects from KhanAcademy.org; entertain yourself by watching and learning from YouTube.com; keep up with technology; when in doubt google it or get a second opinion; do everything legal; keep in touch with relatives; former friends and classmates; stay courageous in the face of adversities, having faith you will withstand the "storm" or difficulties of life, do not lose hope, stay composed, face the problem head on and accept the consequences of your situation, and with the passage of time things will get better; keep good relationship and stay away from toxic relationship and dysfunctional living; learn and understand the 12-step meeting; own your fault and acknowledge your mistake; say you are sorry and mean it; do not be too proud to ask for help; count your blessing every day; take care of your monthly financial responsibilities; have savings, emergency funds good for at least a year, have investments and have a nest egg for your retirement; have a life and disability insurance: pay your taxes on time; celebrate special events; have a regular dental and medical check-up; have a regular doctor, a dentist, an accountant and a lawyer; keep records of important events; be sure to pray and meditate every night; make a monthly lists of things that you are thankful for and have daily gratitude attitude; be respectful and kind to others; be mindful of others; be tolerant of people different from you; be kind, humble, generous and share your wisdom and professional knowledge with your family; never dishonor your family and be the best role model to your children. Share these words of wisdom with family or friends or somebody you love and care. I wish you a blessed, happy, healthy, peaceful and a successful life.

Antonio P. Serrano博士 "過簡單的生活" 我通過以下幾年學習並引導我度過生活：活在當下；熱愛你的工作，為你的工作感到自豪；有內在的力量；包圍你自己與夢想家和積極的人；自我依賴和足智多謀；獲得7-8小時的夜間睡眠；有營養的DASH或地中海飲食，並保持理想的體重；每天步行或鍛煉30分鐘；避免含酒精飲料，絕不吸煙，不要使用非法上癮的藥物；過一個愉快的一天和一個精神週末；盡可能地帶上你的iPhone或安卓手機，學習自我防衛，避免危險的情況和地點；在限速內駕駛；確保你的車是安全的可靠；服用日常補充劑，維生素和處方藥；學習心肺復蘇術和急救；積極的心理愉快態度；保持你的地方清潔整潔，每天晚上洗碗；回收用過的塑料和紙張；學習n烹飪；學習演奏樂器；有興趣愛好或參加體育運動；學習外語；照顧好寵物；閱讀關於成功男士和女士的故事；每天讀好勵志書；練習什麼是道德的；知道你的合法權利；有時候，最好是快樂而不是正確；了解你的個人空間和個人界限；做好準備迎接生活中的任何事情並做好你的功課；保持強大的家庭和社區關係；避免有關宗教，政治和金錢的爭論；志願者為慈善事業；捐贈舊衣服給慈善機構；保持責任心，忠於自己；為慈善和教會貢獻一些時間和經濟上的幫助；旅行到你最喜歡的地方；欣賞精彩的節目；跟上時事；有教育，技能或才能；繼續每天學習新的東西；從InstantTravelLinks.com學習美麗的地方，看看世界；閱讀並複習KhanAcademy.org的一些高中和大學科目；通過觀看和學習YouTube.com娛樂自己；跟上技術；如果有疑問，可以穀歌或獲得第二個意見；盡一切合法；與老親友保持聯繫；朋友和同學；保持良好的關係，遠離毒性關係和功能失調的生活；學習和理解12步會議；擁有你的錯，並承認你的錯誤；說你是對不起，並表示它；不要太驕傲，不要求助；每天計算你的祝福；照顧你每月的財務責任；有儲蓄，應急基金至少一年有效，有投資並且有退休儲備金；有生命和殘疾保險：按時交稅；慶祝特別活動；定期進行牙科和體檢檢查；有正規醫生，牙醫，會計師和律師；保留重要事件的記錄；一定要每晚祈禱和冥想；每月列出你感恩的事情，並且每天都有感激的態度；尊重他人，善待他人；注意別人；容忍與你不同的人；善良，謙虛，慷慨，與家人分享你的智慧和專業知識；永遠不要羞辱你的家人，成為你孩子最好的榜樣。與家人或朋友分享這些智慧的話，或與你愛護的人分享。祝你幸福，快樂，健康，平安，成功。

"Live a simple life " by Antonio P. Serrano, MD. I have learned through the years the following and has guided me through life: Live in the moment; love your job and be proud of your work; have internal strength; surround yourself with dreamers and positive people; be self-reliant and be resourceful; get 7-8 hour nightly sleep; have a nutritious DASH or Mediterranean diet and maintain an ideal weight; have a daily 30 minute walk or exercise; avoid alcoholic drinks, never smoke and never use illegal addictive drugs ; have an enjoyable day and a spiritual weekend; as much as possible have your iPhone or android phone with you, learn self-defense and avoid dangerous situation and places; drive within the speed limit; make sure your car is safe and dependable; take your daily supplements, vitamins and prescription medicines; learn CPR and First Aid; have positive mental happy attitude; keep your place clean and organized and wash your dishes every night; recycle used plastics and papers; learn cooking; learn to play a musical instrument; have a hobby or participate in sport; learn a foreign language; take good care of a pet; read stories about successful men and women; read good inspirational book every day; practice what is ethical; know your legal rights; sometimes it is better to be happy than right; know your personal space and personal boundaries; be prepared for anything that life throws at you and do your homework; maintain a strong family and community ties; avoid arguments about religion, politics and money; volunteer for charitable causes; donate used clothes to charity; stay responsible and true to yourself; contribute some time and financial help to charity and church; travel to your favorite places; enjoy a good show; keep up with current events; have an education, skills or talents; continue to learn something new every day; learn beautiful places from InstantTravelLinks. com and see the world; read and review some high school and college subjects from KhanAcademy.org; entertain yourself by watching and learning from YouTube.com; keep up with technology; when in doubt google it or get a second opinion; do everything legal; keep in touch with relatives; former friends and classmates; stay courageous in the face of adversities, having faith you will withstand the "storm" or difficulties of life, do not lose hope, stay composed, face the problem head on and accept the consequences of your situation, and with the passage of time things will get better; keep good relationship and stay away from toxic relationship and dysfunctional living; learn and understand the 12-step meeting; own your fault and acknowledge your mistake; say you are sorry and mean it; do not be too proud to ask for help; count your blessing every day; take care of your monthly financial responsibilities; have savings, emergency funds good for at least a year, have investments and have a nest egg for your retirement; have a life and disability insurance: pay your taxes on time; celebrate special events; have a regular dental and medical check-up; have a regular doctor, a dentist, an accountant and a lawyer; keep records of important events; be sure to pray and meditate every night; make a monthly lists of things that you are thankful for and have daily gratitude attitude; be respectful and kind to others; be mindful of others; be tolerant of people different from you; be kind, humble, generous and share your wisdom and professional knowledge with your family; never dishonor your family and be the best role model to your children. Share these words of wisdom with family or friends or somebody you love and care. I wish you a blessed, happy, healthy, peaceful and a successful life.

Lebe ein einfaches Leben "von Antonio P. Serrano, MD. Ich habe durch die folgenden Jahre gelernt und mich durch das Leben geführt: Lebe in dem Moment; Liebe deinen Job und sei stolz auf deine Arbeit; innere Stärke haben; Umgib dich mit Träumern und positiven Menschen; selbstständig sein und einfallsreich sein; 7-8 Stunden nächtlichen Schlaf bekommen; eine nahrhafte DASH- oder Mittelmeerdiät haben und ein ideales Gewicht beibehalten; täglich 30 Minuten laufen oder trainieren; Vermeiden Sie alkoholische Getränke, rauchen Sie niemals und benutzen Sie niemals illegale Suchtmittel; einen schönen Tag und ein spirituelles Wochenende haben; so viel wie möglich haben Sie Ihr iPhone oder Android-Handy mit Ihnen, lernen Selbstverteidigung und vermeiden gefährliche Situationen und Orte; Fahrt innerhalb der Geschwindigkeitsbegrenzung; stellen Sie sicher, dass Ihr Auto sicher und zuverlässig ist; nehmen Sie Ihre täglichen Ergänzungen, Vitamine und verschreibungspflichtige Medikamente; lerne HLW und Erste Hilfe; habe positive geistige glückliche Einstellung; Halten Sie Ihren Platz sauber und organisiert und waschen Sie Ihre Gerichte jede Nacht; Recycling von gebrauchten Kunststoffen und Papieren; Kochen lernen; lerne ein Musikinstrument zu spielen; ein Hobby haben oder am Sport teilnehmen; lerne eine Fremdsprache; achte gut auf ein Haustier; Lesen Sie Geschichten über erfolgreiche Männer und Frauen; lese jeden Tag ein gutes inspirierendes Buch; übe, was ethisch ist; kenne deine gesetzlichen Rechte; Manchmal ist es besser, glücklich zu sein als richtig. kenne deinen persönlichen Raum und deine persönlichen Grenzen; Sei bereit für alles, was das Leben dir zuwirft und mache deine Hausaufgaben; Aufrechterhaltung einer starken familiären und gesellschaftlichen Bindung; vermeiden Sie Argumente über Religion, Politik und Geld; Freiwillige für wohltätige Zwecke; alte Kleider für wohltätige Zwecke spenden; bleib verantwortlich und treu zu dir selbst; Spende etwas Zeit und finanzielle Hilfe für Wohltätigkeit und Kirche; zu deinen Lieblingsplätzen reisen; genieße eine gute Show; Schritt halten mit aktuellen Ereignissen; eine Ausbildung, Fähigkeiten oder Talente haben; weiter lernen etwas Neues jeden Tag; lerne wunderschöne Orte von InstantTravelLinks.com und entdecke die Welt; Lesen und überprüfen Sie einige High School und College Themen von KhanAcademy.org; unterhalten Sie sich, indem Sie YouTube.com ansehen und von ihm lernen. Schritt halten mit Technologie; im Zweifelsfall googeln oder eine zweite Meinung einholen; mach alles legal; Bleiben Sie in Kontakt mit alten Verwandten; Freunde und Klassenkameraden; Bleibe mutig im Angesicht von Widrigkeiten, habe Vertrauen, dass du dem "Sturm" oder den Schwierigkeiten des Lebens standhalten wirst, verliere die Hoffnung nicht, bleib ruhig, stelle dich dem Problem gegenüber und akzeptiere die Konsequenzen deiner Situation und im Laufe der Zeit die Dinge es wird besser; Halte eine gute Beziehung und halte dich von giftigen Beziehungen und dysfunktionalem Leben fern. lerne und verstehe das 12-stufige Treffen; Besitze deine Schuld und erkenne deinen Fehler an; sagen Sie, es tut mir leid und meine es ernst; Sei nicht zu stolz, um Hilfe zu bitten. zähle jeden Tag deinen Segen; kümmern Sie sich um Ihre monatlichen finanziellen Verantwortlichkeiten; Ersparnisse, Notstandsfonds mindestens ein Jahr lang, haben Investitionen und haben ein Nest Ei für Ihren Ruhestand; eine Lebens- und Berufsunfähigkeitsversicherung haben: zahlen Sie Ihre Steuern rechtzeitig; besondere Ereignisse feiern; regelmäßig eine zahnärztliche und medizinische Untersuchung durchführen lassen; einen ordentlichen Arzt, einen Zahnarzt, einen Buchhalter und einen Rechtsanwalt haben; Aufzeichnungen über wichtige Ereignisse führen; Achten Sie darauf, jede Nacht zu beten und zu meditieren; mache monatliche Listen von Dingen, für die du dankbar bist und habe täglich Dankbarkeitshaltung; sei respektvoll und freundlich zu anderen; Achte auf andere. sei tolerant gegenüber Menschen, die sich von dir unterscheiden; Sei freundlich, bescheiden, großzügig und teile deine Weisheit und dein Fachwissen mit deiner Familie; Schande niemals über deine Familie und sei das beste Vorbild für deine Kinder. Teilen Sie diese Worte der Weisheit mit Familie oder Freunden oder jemandem, den Sie lieben und sich interessieren. Ich wünsche Ihnen ein gesegnetes, glückliches, gesundes, friedliches und erfolgreiches Leben.

"Live a simple life " by Antonio P. Serrano, MD. I have learned through the years the following and has guided me through life: Live in the moment; love your job and be proud of your work; have internal strength; surround yourself with dreamers and positive people; be self-reliant and be resourceful; get 7-8 hour nightly sleep; have a nutritious DASH or Mediterranean diet and maintain an ideal weight; have a daily 30 minute walk or exercise; avoid alcoholic drinks, never smoke and never use illegal addictive drugs ; have an enjoyable day and a spiritual weekend; as much as possible have your iPhone or android phone with you, learn self-defense and avoid dangerous situation and places; drive within the speed limit; make sure your car is safe and dependable; take your daily supplements, vitamins and prescription medicines; learn CPR and First Aid; have positive mental happy attitude; keep your place clean and organized and wash your dishes every night; recycle used plastics and papers; learn cooking; learn to play a musical instrument; have a hobby or participate in sport; learn a foreign language; take good care of a pet; read stories about successful men and women; read good inspirational book every day; practice what is ethical; know your legal rights; sometimes it is better to be happy than right; know your personal space and personal boundaries; be prepared for anything that life throws at you and do your homework; maintain a strong family and community ties; avoid arguments about religion, politics and money; volunteer for charitable causes; donate used clothes to charity; stay responsible and true to yourself; contribute some time and financial help to charity and church; travel to your favorite places; enjoy a good show; keep up with current events; have an education, skills or talents; continue to learn something new every day; learn beautiful places from InstantTravelLinks. com and see the world; read and review some high school and college subjects from KhanAcademy.org; entertain yourself by watching and learning from YouTube.com; keep up with technology; when in doubt google it or get a second opinion; do everything legal; keep in touch with relatives; former friends and classmates; stay courageous in the face of adversities, having faith you will withstand the "storm" or difficulties of life, do not lose hope, stay composed, face the problem head on and accept the consequences of your situation, and with the passage of time things will get better; keep good relationship and stay away from toxic relationship and dysfunctional living; learn and understand the 12-step meeting; own your fault and acknowledge your mistake; say you are sorry and mean it; do not be too proud to ask for help; count your blessing every day; take care of your monthly financial responsibilities; have savings, emergency funds good for at least a year, have investments and have a nest egg for your retirement; have a life and disability insurance: pay your taxes on time; celebrate special events; have a regular dental and medical check-up; have a regular doctor, a dentist, an accountant and a lawyer; keep records of important events; be sure to pray and meditate every night; make a monthly lists of things that you are thankful for and have daily gratitude attitude; be respectful and kind to others; be mindful of others; be tolerant of people different from you; be kind, humble, generous and share your wisdom and professional knowledge with your family; never dishonor your family and be the best role model to your children. Share these words of wisdom with family or friends or somebody you love and care. I wish you a blessed, happy, healthy, peaceful and a successful life.

«Живи простой жизнью» Антонио П. Серрано, доктор медицины. Я узнал через годы следующее и руководил жизнью: живи в данный момент: любишь свою работу и гордишься своей работой, обладаешь внутренней силой, окружай себя с мечтателями и позитивными людьми, быть уверенными в себе и быть находчивыми, получать 7-8-часовой ночной сон, иметь питательную диету DASH или средиземноморскую диету и поддерживать идеальный вес, ежедневно совершать 30 минут ходьбы или заниматься спортом, избегать алкогольных напитков, никогда не курить и никогда не используйте противозаконные наркотики, наслаждайтесь приятным днем и духовным уик-эндом, насколько возможно у вас есть ваш iPhone или Android-телефон, изучите самооборону и избегайте опасной ситуации и мест, двигайтесь в пределах ограничения скорости, убедитесь, что ваш автомобиль безопасен и надежно, принимать ваши ежедневные добавки, витамины и лекарства, отпускаемые по рецепту, изучать СЛР и первую помощь, иметь позитивное умственное настроение, держать свое место в чистоте, организовывать и мыть посуду каждую ночь, перерабатывать использованные пластмассы и бумаги, п приготовление пищи; научиться играть на музыкальном инструменте; иметь хобби или участвовать в спорте; изучать иностранный язык; заботиться о домашнем животном; читать истории об успешных мужчинах и женщинах; читать хорошую вдохновляющую книгу каждый день; практика, что этично; знать свои законные права; иногда лучше быть счастливым, чем правым; знать свое личное пространство и личные границы; будьте готовы ко всему, что жизнь бросает на вас и делает домашнее задание; поддерживать крепкие семейные и общественные связи; избегать споров о религии, политике и деньгах; добровольцем по благотворительным причинам; пожертвовать старую одежду на благотворительность; оставаться ответственным и верным себе; внести некоторое время и финансовую помощь в благотворительность и церковь; отправляйтесь в свои любимые места; наслаждайтесь хорошим шоу; следить за текущими событиями; иметь образование, навыки или таланты; продолжать изучать что-то новое каждый день; изучать красивые места из сайта InstantTravelLinks.com и видеть мир; читать и просматривать некоторые предметы средней школы и колледжа от KhanAcademy.org; развлекайтесь, наблюдая и участвуя в YouTube.com; не отставать от технологий, таких как 3D-печать; Robotics; Nano Technology; Терапия стволовыми клетками; Генетическая инженерия и искусственный интеллект; когда в сомнении google это или получить второе мнение; делать все законным; поддерживать связь со старыми родственниками; друзей и одноклассников; оставайтесь мужественными перед лицом невзгод, имея веру, вы будете противостоять «шторму» или трудностям жизни, не терять надежду, оставаться в составе, сталкиваться с проблемой и принимать последствия своей ситуации, а с течением времени вещи станет лучше; поддерживать хорошие отношения и избегать токсичных отношений и дисфункциональной жизни; изучить и понять 12-ступенчатое совещание; владейте своей ошибкой и подтвердите свою ошибку; скажите, что вы сожалеете и имеете в виду это; не будьте слишком горды, чтобы просить о помощи; посчитайте свое благословение каждый день; заботиться о своих ежемесячных финансовых обязанностях; имеют сбережения, чрезвычайные фонды, имеющие хорошую прибыль не менее года, имеют инвестиции и имеют гнездовое яйцо для вашего выхода на пенсию; имеют страхование жизни и инвалидности: своевременно оплачивать налоги; праздновать специальные мероприятия; иметь регулярный стоматологический и медицинский осмотр; иметь постоянного врача, дантиста, бухгалтера и адвоката; вести учет важных событий; не забудьте молиться и медитировать каждую ночь; составлять ежемесячные списки вещей, за которые вы благодарны, и иметь ежедневную благодарность; быть уважительным и добрым к другим; помнить о других; быть терпимым к людям, отличным от вас; быть добрым, скромным, щедрым и делиться своей мудростью и профессиональными знаниями с семьей; никогда не обесчестите свою семью и не станете лучшей образцовой моделью для своих детей. Поделитесь этими словами мудрости с семьей или друзьями или с кем-то, кого вы любите и заботитесь. Желаю вам благословенной, счастливой, здоровой, мирной и успешной жизни.

"Live a simple life " by Antonio P. Serrano, MD. I have learned through the years the following and has guided me through life: Live in the moment; love your job and be proud of your work; have internal strength; surround yourself with dreamers and positive people; be self-reliant and be resourceful; get 7-8 hour nightly sleep; have a nutritious DASH or Mediterranean diet and maintain an ideal weight; have a daily 30 minute walk or exercise; avoid alcoholic drinks, never smoke and never use illegal addictive drugs ; have an enjoyable day and a spiritual weekend; as much as possible have your iPhone or android phone with you, learn self-defense and avoid dangerous situation and places; drive within the speed limit; make sure your car is safe and dependable; take your daily supplements, vitamins and prescription medicines; learn CPR and First Aid; have positive mental happy attitude; keep your place clean and organized and wash your dishes every night; recycle used plastics and papers; learn cooking; learn to play a musical instrument; have a hobby or participate in sport; learn a foreign language; take good care of a pet; read stories about successful men and women; read good inspirational book every day; practice what is ethical; know your legal rights; sometimes it is better to be happy than right; know your personal space and personal boundaries; be prepared for anything that life throws at you and do your homework; maintain a strong family and community ties; avoid arguments about religion, politics and money; volunteer for charitable causes; donate used clothes to charity; stay responsible and true to yourself; contribute some time and financial help to charity and church; travel to your favorite places; enjoy a good show; keep up with current events; have an education, skills or talents; continue to learn something new every day; learn beautiful places from InstantTravelLinks. com and see the world; read and review some high school and college subjects from KhanAcademy.org; entertain yourself by watching and learning from YouTube.com; keep up with technology; when in doubt google it or get a second opinion; do everything legal; keep in touch with relatives; former friends and classmates; stay courageous in the face of adversities, having faith you will withstand the "storm" or difficulties of life, do not lose hope, stay composed, face the problem head on and accept the consequences of your situation, and with the passage of time things will get better; keep good relationship and stay away from toxic relationship and dysfunctional living; learn and understand the 12-step meeting; own your fault and acknowledge your mistake; say you are sorry and mean it; do not be too proud to ask for help; count your blessing every day; take care of your monthly financial responsibilities; have savings, emergency funds good for at least a year, have investments and have a nest egg for your retirement; have a life and disability insurance: pay your taxes on time; celebrate special events; have a regular dental and medical check-up; have a regular doctor, a dentist, an accountant and a lawyer; keep records of important events; be sure to pray and meditate every night; make a monthly lists of things that you are thankful for and have daily gratitude attitude; be respectful and kind to others; be mindful of others; be tolerant of people different from you; be kind, humble, generous and share your wisdom and professional knowledge with your family; never dishonor your family and be the best role model to your children. Share these words of wisdom with family or friends or somebody you love and care. I wish you a blessed, happy, healthy, peaceful and a successful life.

Vivez une vie simple »par Antonio P. Serrano, MD. Au cours des années, j'ai appris les choses suivantes et m'a guidé tout au long de ma vie: vis le moment présent; aime ton travail et sois fier de ton travail; avoir une force interne; Entourez-vous de rêveurs et de personnes positives; être autonome et débrouillard; dormez 7 à 8 heures par nuit; avoir un régime nutritif DASH ou méditerranéen et maintenir un poids idéal; faire une promenade ou un exercice quotidien de 30 minutes; éviter les boissons alcoolisées, ne jamais fumer et ne jamais utiliser de drogues addictives illégales; passez une journée agréable et un week-end spirituel; Autant que possible, ayez votre iPhone ou votre téléphone Android avec vous, apprenez à vous défendre et évitez les situations et les lieux dangereux; conduire dans les limites de vitesse; assurez-vous que votre voiture est sûre et fiable; prenez vos suppléments quotidiens, vos vitamines et vos médicaments sur ordonnance; apprendre la RCR et les premiers soins; avoir une attitude mentale positive et heureuse; gardez votre place propre et bien rangée et lavez votre vaisselle tous les soirs; recycler les plastiques et papiers usés; apprendre à cuisiner; apprendre à jouer d'un instrument de musique; avoir un passe-temps ou participer à un sport; Apprenez une langue étrangère; prendre bien soin d'un animal de compagnie; lire des histoires d'hommes et de femmes qui ont réussi; lire un bon livre d'inspiration tous les jours; pratiquer ce qui est éthique; connaître vos droits légaux; parfois, il vaut mieux être heureux que juste; connaître votre espace personnel et vos limites personnelles; soyez prêt à tout ce que la vie vous jette et faites vos devoirs; maintenir des liens familiaux et communautaires solides; éviter les disputes sur la religion, la politique et l'argent; faire du bénévolat pour des œuvres de bienfaisance; faire don de vieux vêtements à des œuvres de charité; rester responsable et fidèle à soi-même; consacrer du temps et une aide financière à des œuvres caritatives et à l'église; voyager à vos endroits préférés; profiter d'un bon spectacle; suivre l'actualité; avoir une éducation, des compétences ou des talents; continuer à apprendre quelque chose de nouveau chaque jour; apprendre de beaux endroits de InstantTravelLinks.com et voir le monde; lire et relire certaines matières des lycées et collèges de KhanAcademy.org; divertissez-vous en regardant et en apprenant sur YouTube.com; suivre la technologie; en cas de doute, recherchez-le sur Google ou obtenez un deuxième avis; faire tout ce qui est légal; rester en contact avec les anciens parents; amis et camarades de classe; restez courageux face aux épreuves, ayez la foi, vous ferez face à la «tempête» ou aux difficultés de la vie, ne perdez pas espoir, restez calme, faites face au problème et acceptez les conséquences de votre situation, et avec le passage du temps va aller mieux; maintenir de bonnes relations et rester à l'écart des relations toxiques et des modes de vie dysfonctionnels; apprendre et comprendre la réunion en 12 étapes; reconnaissez votre faute et reconnaissez votre erreur; dites que vous êtes désolé et que vous le pensez ne soyez pas trop fier pour demander de l'aide; comptez chaque jour votre bénédiction; prendre soin de vos responsabilités financières mensuelles; avoir des économies, des fonds d'urgence valables pendant au moins un an, avoir des investissements et avoir un pécule pour votre retraite; avoir une assurance vie et invalidité: payez vos impôts à temps; célébrer des événements spéciaux; passer régulièrement un examen dentaire et médical; avoir un médecin régulier, un dentiste, un comptable et un avocat; tenir des registres d'événements importants; veillez à prier et à méditer chaque nuit; faites une liste mensuelle des choses pour lesquelles vous êtes reconnaissant et qui ont une attitude de gratitude quotidienne; être respectueux et gentil avec les autres; être attentif aux autres; soyez tolérant envers des personnes différentes de vous; soyez gentil, humble, généreux et partagez votre sagesse et vos connaissances professionnelles avec votre famille; ne déshonorez jamais votre famille et soyez le meilleur modèle pour vos enfants. Partagez ces paroles de sagesse avec votre famille, vos amis ou une personne que vous aimez et aimez. Je vous souhaite une vie bénie, heureuse, saine, paisible et prospère.

"Live a simple life " by Antonio P. Serrano, MD. I have learned through the years the following and has guided me through life: Live in the moment; love your job and be proud of your work; have internal strength; surround yourself with dreamers and positive people; be self-reliant and be resourceful; get 7-8 hour nightly sleep; have a nutritious DASH or Mediterranean diet and maintain an ideal weight; have a daily 30 minute walk or exercise; avoid alcoholic drinks, never smoke and never use illegal addictive drugs ; have an enjoyable day and a spiritual weekend; as much as possible have your iPhone or android phone with you, learn self-defense and avoid dangerous situation and places; drive within the speed limit; make sure your car is safe and dependable; take your daily supplements, vitamins and prescription medicines; learn CPR and First Aid; have positive mental happy attitude; keep your place clean and organized and wash your dishes every night; recycle used plastics and papers; learn cooking; learn to play a musical instrument; have a hobby or participate in sport; learn a foreign language; take good care of a pet; read stories about successful men and women; read good inspirational book every day; practice what is ethical; know your legal rights; sometimes it is better to be happy than right; know your personal space and personal boundaries; be prepared for anything that life throws at you and do your homework; maintain a strong family and community ties; avoid arguments about religion, politics and money; volunteer for charitable causes; donate used clothes to charity; stay responsible and true to yourself; contribute some time and financial help to charity and church; travel to your favorite places; enjoy a good show; keep up with current events; have an education, skills or talents; continue to learn something new every day; learn beautiful places from InstantTravelLinks. com and see the world; read and review some high school and college subjects from KhanAcademy.org; entertain yourself by watching and learning from YouTube.com; keep up with technology; when in doubt google it or get a second opinion; do everything legal; keep in touch with relatives; former friends and classmates; stay courageous in the face of adversities, having faith you will withstand the "storm" or difficulties of life, do not lose hope, stay composed, face the problem head on and accept the consequences of your situation, and with the passage of time things will get better; keep good relationship and stay away from toxic relationship and dysfunctional living; learn and understand the 12-step meeting; own your fault and acknowledge your mistake; say you are sorry and mean it; do not be too proud to ask for help; count your blessing every day; take care of your monthly financial responsibilities; have savings, emergency funds good for at least a year, have investments and have a nest egg for your retirement; have a life and disability insurance: pay your taxes on time; celebrate special events; have a regular dental and medical check-up; have a regular doctor, a dentist, an accountant and a lawyer; keep records of important events; be sure to pray and meditate every night; make a monthly lists of things that you are thankful for and have daily gratitude attitude; be respectful and kind to others; be mindful of others; be tolerant of people different from you; be kind, humble, generous and share your wisdom and professional knowledge with your family; never dishonor your family and be the best role model to your children. Share these words of wisdom with family or friends or somebody you love and care. I wish you a blessed, happy, healthy, peaceful and a successful life.

"Live a simple life " by Antonio P. Serrano, MD. I have learned through the years the following and has guided me through life: Live in the moment; love your job and be proud of your work; have internal strength; surround yourself with dreamers and positive people; be self-reliant and be resourceful; get 7-8 hour nightly sleep; have a nutritious DASH or Mediterranean diet and maintain an ideal weight; have a daily 30 minute walk or exercise; avoid alcoholic drinks, never smoke and never use illegal addictive drugs ; have an enjoyable day and a spiritual weekend; as much as possible have your iPhone or android phone with you, learn self-defense and avoid dangerous situation and places; drive within the speed limit; make sure your car is safe and dependable; take your daily supplements, vitamins and prescription medicines; learn CPR and First Aid; have positive mental happy attitude; keep your place clean and organized and wash your dishes every night; recycle used plastics and papers; learn cooking; learn to play a musical instrument; have a hobby or participate in sport; learn a foreign language; take good care of a pet; read stories about successful men and women; read good inspirational book every day; practice what is ethical; know your legal rights; sometimes it is better to be happy than right; know your personal space and personal boundaries; be prepared for anything that life throws at you and do your homework; maintain a strong family and community ties; avoid arguments about religion, politics and money; volunteer for charitable causes; donate used clothes to charity; stay responsible and true to yourself; contribute some time and financial help to charity and church; travel to your favorite places; enjoy a good show; keep up with current events; have an education, skills or talents; continue to learn something new every day; learn beautiful places from InstantTravelLinks. com and see the world; read and review some high school and college subjects from KhanAcademy.org; entertain yourself by watching and learning from YouTube.com; keep up with technology; when in doubt google it or get a second opinion; do everything legal; keep in touch with relatives; former friends and classmates; stay courageous in the face of adversities, having faith you will withstand the "storm" or difficulties of life, do not lose hope, stay composed, face the problem head on and accept the consequences of your situation, and with the passage of time things will get better; keep good relationship and stay away from toxic relationship and dysfunctional living; learn and understand the 12-step meeting; own your fault and acknowledge your mistake; say you are sorry and mean it; do not be too proud to ask for help; count your blessing every day; take care of your monthly financial responsibilities; have savings, emergency funds good for at least a year, have investments and have a nest egg for your retirement; have a life and disability insurance: pay your taxes on time; celebrate special events; have a regular dental and medical check-up; have a regular doctor, a dentist, an accountant and a lawyer; keep records of important events; be sure to pray and meditate every night; make a monthly lists of things that you are thankful for and have daily gratitude attitude; be respectful and kind to others; be mindful of others; be tolerant of people different from you; be kind, humble, generous and share your wisdom and professional knowledge with your family; never dishonor your family and be the best role model to your children. Share these words of wisdom with family or friends or somebody you love and care. I wish you a blessed, happy, healthy, peaceful and a successful life.

ETIQUETTE

Etiquette is a code of behavior that delineates expectations for social behavior according to contemporary conventional norms within a society, social class, or group. The French word étiquette, literally signifying a tag or label, was used in a modern sense in English around 1750.

https://en.wikipedia.org/wiki/Etiquette

Please view the etiquette presented by Bright Side on Youtube.com

THERE ARE 3 KINDS OF PEOPLE YOU WILL ENCOUNTER IN YOUR LIFE.

---

1. *THERE ARE PEOPLE WHO WILL NOT AFFECT OUR LIVES.*

2. *THERE WILL BE PEOPLE WHO WILL BE A BLESSING TO OUR LIVES.*

3. *THERE WILL BE PEOPLE WHO WILL BECOME A LESSON TO OUR LIVES. THESE UNFORTUNATE SOULS WILL TEACH US TO AVOID SITUATIONS THAT MAKE THEM THE WAY THEY ARE. LEARN FROM THEM BUT DO NOT LET THEM "CONTAMINATE" YOUR PERSONALITY AND BEHAVIOR. MINIMIZE YOU ASSOCIATION WITH THEM.*

LIMIT YOUR ASSOCIATION WITH THESE PEOPLE.

1. *Two Faced People – These are people who say nice things in front of you, but as soon as you turn around they say bad things about you. They are usually opinionated and judgmental.*
2. *Dishonest people – These are people who cannot be honest about a situation. They muddle the truth and play games.*
3. *Dysfunctional people – These are people who are hard to get along with. They have issues with their personality. Usually they are living with toxic people or have addictive behavior.*
4. *Pessimistic people - These are people who are depressed and see the world negatively. Nothing works for them, they like drama in life. They believe in Doom and Gloom.*
5. *Manipulators and Control Freaks – These are people who make you believe in things but with their own ulterior motives. They want to consume you from doing things opposed to your beliefs and principles. They are control freaks; they want to do things without asking suggestions from anybody. It's their way or the highway.*

Do not let these people contaminate you. Let them be a lesson to you.

What Is The Dash Diet

The healthy DASH Diet was developed to lower blood pressure without medication. Numerous of studies have shown that DASH Diet reduces the risk of many diseases like diabetes, heart diseases, cancer, stroke, and kidney stones. It has proven to be an effective way to lose weight and become healthier at the same time.

What Is The Mediterranean Diet

It's a heart healthy diet that includes the food staples of people who live in the region around the Mediterranean Sea, such as Greece, Croatia and Italy. This diet is rich in fruits and vegetables, whole grains, seafood, nuts, legumes and olive oil. You'll limit or avoid red meat, sugary food and diary.

IDEAL WEIGHT

If your weight is above that the ideal weight for you height on the charts, it is tempting to think it is because you are lean but muscular. Very muscular people may have a higher body mass index while still having low body fat. Meanwhile, people who have lost muscle and replace it with fat may appear to have a normal BMI when they actually have too much body fat and not enough muscle for good health outcomes.

Ideal Weight

Height	Weight		
	Normal	**Overweight**	**Obese**
4' 10"	91 to 118 lbs.	119 to 142 lbs.	143 to 186 lbs.
4' 11"	94 to 123 lbs.	124 to 147 lbs.	148 to 193 lbs.
5'	97 to 127 lbs.	128 to 152 lbs.	153 to 199 lbs.
5' 1"	100 to 131 lbs.	132 to 157 lbs.	158 to 206 lbs.
5' 2"	104 to 135 lbs.	136 to 163 lbs.	164 to 213 lbs.
5' 3"	107 to 140 lbs.	141 to 168 lbs.	169 to 220 lbs.
5' 4"	110 to 144 lbs.	145 to 173 lbs.	174 to 227 lbs.
5' 5"	114 to 149 lbs.	150 to 179 lbs.	180 to 234 lbs.
5' 6"	118 to 154 lbs.	155 to 185 lbs.	186 to 241 lbs.
5' 7"	121 to 158 lbs.	159 to 190 lbs.	191 to 249 lbs.
5' 8"	125 to 163 lbs.	164 to 196 lbs.	197 to 256 lbs.
5' 9"	128 to 168 lbs.	169 to 202 lbs.	203 to 263 lbs.
5' 10"	132 to 173 lbs.	174 to 208 lbs.	209 to 271 lbs.
5' 11"	136 to 178 lbs.	179 to 214 lbs.	215 to 279 lbs.
6'	140 to 183 lbs.	184 to 220 lbs.	221 to 287 lbs.
6' 1"	144 to 188 lbs.	189 to 226 lbs.	227 to 295 lbs.
6' 2"	148 to 193 lbs.	194 to 232 lbs.	233 to 303 lbs.
6' 3"	152 to 199 lbs.	200 to 239 lbs.	240 to 311 lbs.
6' 4"	156 to 204 lbs.	205 to 245 lbs.	246 to 320 lbs.
BMI	19 to 24	25 to 29	30 to 39

WHAT IS BODY MASS INDEX?

The amount of fat is the critical measurements. A good indicator of how much fat you can carry is the body mass index (BMI). Although it is not a perfect measure, it gives a fairly accurate assessment of how much of your body is composed of fat.

VITAL SIGNS

Vital signs reflect essential body functions, including your heartbeat, breathing rate, temperature, and blood pressure. Your health care provider may watch, measure, or monitor your vital signs to check your level of physical functioning. Normal vital signs change with age, sex, weight, exercise capability, and overall health.

Normal vital sign ranges for the average healthy adult while resting are:

Blood pressure: 90/60 mm Hg to 120/80 mm Hg

Breathing: 12 to 18 breaths per minute

Pulse: 60 to 100 beats per minute

Temperature: 97.8°F to 99.1°F (36.5°C to 37.3°C)/average 98.6°F (37°C)

https://medlineplus.gov/ency/article/002341.htm

Pediatrics
for Medical
Students

Pediatric Vital Signs Reference Chart

This table, along with our detailed references can be found online at http://www.pedscases.com/pediatric-vital-signs-reference-chart. For a more detailed approach to this topic, see our podcast on "Pediatric Vital Signs."

Heart Rate

Normal Heart Rate by Age (beats/minute)
Reference: PALS Guidelines, 2015

Age	Awake Rate	Sleeping Rate
Neonate (<28 d)	100-205	90-160
Infant (1 mo-1 y)	100-190	90-160
Toddler (1-2 y)	98-140	80-120
Preschool (3-5 y)	80-120	65-100
School-age (6-11 y)	75-118	58-90
Adolescent (12-15 y)	60-100	50-90

Respiratory Rate

Normal Respiratory Rate by Age (breaths/minute)
Reference: PALS Guidelines, 2015

Age	Normal Respiratory Rate
Infants (<1 y)	30-53
Toddler (1-2 y)	22-37
Preschool (3-5 y)	20-28
School-age (6-11 y)	18-25
Adolescent (12-15 y)	12-20

Blood Pressure

Normal Blood Pressure by Age (mm Hg)
Reference: PALS Guidelines, 2015

Age	Systolic Pressure	Diastolic Pressure	Systolic Hypotension
Birth (12 h, <1000 g)	39-59	16-36	<40-50
Birth (12 h, 3 kg)	60-76	31-45	<50
Neonate (96 h)	67-84	35-53	<60
Infant (1-12 mo)	72-104	37-56	<70
Toddler (1-2 y)	86-106	42-63	<70 + (age in years x 2)
Preschooler (3-5 y)	89-112	46-72	<70 + (age in years x 2)
School-age (6-9 y)	97-115	57-76	<70 + (age in years x 2)
Preadolescent (10-11 y)	102-120	61-80	<90
Adolescent (12-15 y)	110-131	64-83	<90

For diagnosis of hypertension refer to the 2017 AAP guidelines Table 4 and 5:
http://pediatrics.aappublications.org/content/early/2017/08/21/peds.2017-1904.

Temperature

Normal Temperature Range by Method
Reference: CPS Position Statement on Temperature Measurement in Pediatrics, 2015

Method	Temperature (°C)
Rectal	36.6-38
Ear	35.8-38
Oral	35.5-37.5
Axillary	36.5-37.5

Temperature ranges do not vary with age. Axillary, tympanic and temporal temps for screening (less accurate). Rectal and oral temps for definitive measurement (unless contraindication).

Oxygen Saturation

Normal pediatric pulse oximetry (SPO2) values have not yet been firmly established. SPO2 is lower in the immediate newborn period. Beyond this period, a SPO2 of <92% should be a cause of concern and may suggest a respiratory disease or cyanotic heart disease.

Developed by Dr. Chris Novak and Dr. Peter Gill for PedsCases.com.
July 10, 2018.

BLOOD SUGAR LEVELS

BLOOD SUGAR CHART

FASTING

Normal for person without diabetes	70–99 mg/dl (3.9–5.5 mmol/L)
Official ADA recommendation for someone with diabetes	80–130 mg/dl (4.4–7.2 mmol/L)

2 HOURS AFTER MEALS

Normal for person without diabetes	Less than 140 mg/dl (7.8 mmol/L)
Official ADA recommendation for someone with diabetes	Less than 180 mg/dl (10.0 mmol/L)

HBA1C

Normal for person without diabetes	Less than 5.7%
Official ADA recommendation for someone with diabetes	7.0% or less

MODERN MEDICINE CABINET

Meds Over the Counter

1. *Antacids: Ranitidine, Omeprazole, or Nexium.*

2. *Antihistamine: Claritin, Allegra, Zyrtec, or Benadryl.*

3. *Analgesic: Acetaminophen, Advil, Aleve, or Balm Aspirin*

4. *Cold medication: Mucinex MD*

5. *Antibiotic Ointment: Neosporin*

6. *Antidiarrheal: Imodium AD, Pepto-Bismol, or Laxatives such as Dulcolax, Surfak, Colace and Glycerin Suppositories.*

Medical Equipment

1. *Thermometer*

2. *Glucometer*

3. *Digital BP Machine*

4. *Pulse Oximeter*

Prescribed medication

Must be locked & out of reach of children at all times.

RECOMMENDED LINKS FOR EVERYBODY:

Healthgrades.com

Healthfinder.com

Shopkidde.com

Survivalfrog.com

Docshow.global

Influencer.properties

WebMD.com

5 RECOMMENDED BOOKS

1. *THE POWER OF NOW BY ECKHART TOLLE*

2. *THE POWER OF INTENTION BY ECKHART TOLLE*

3. *ASK AND IT IS GIVEN BY ESTHER AND ABRAHAM HICKS*

4. *DON'T SWEAT THE SMALL STUFF BY RICHARD CARLSON*

5. *MAN'S SEARCH FOR MEANING BY VIKTOR FRANKL*

References

Youtube.com

Khanacademy.org

InstantTravelLinks.com

IMPORTANT TELEPHONE NUMBERS

1. *Poison control: 1-800-222-1222*

2. *Domestic violence: 1-800-799-7233*

3. *Addiction hotline: 1-855-466-7204*

4. *Local Police:* _____

5. *Local Doctor:* _____

Female Chart for Normal Weight

Height			Small Frame					Medium Frame					Large Frame				
(ft)	(in)	(cm)	(lbs)		(lbs)	(kg)		(kg)	(lbs)		(lbs)	(kg)		(kg)	(lbs)		(lbs)	(kg)		(kg)
4	10	147	102	-	111	46	-	50	109	-	121	49	-	55	118	-	131	54	-	59
4	11	150	103	-	113	47	-	51	111	-	123	50	-	56	120	-	134	54	-	61
5	0	153	104	-	115	47	-	52	113	-	126	51	-	57	122	-	137	55	-	62
5	1	155	106	-	118	48	-	54	115	-	129	52	-	59	125	-	140	57	-	64
5	2	158	108	-	121	49	-	55	118	-	132	54	-	60	128	-	143	58	-	65
5	3	160	111	-	124	50	-	56	121	-	135	55	-	61	131	-	147	59	-	67
5	4	163	114	-	127	52	-	58	124	-	138	56	-	63	134	-	151	61	-	68
5	5	165	117	-	130	53	-	59	127	-	141	58	-	64	137	-	155	62	-	70
5	6	168	120	-	133	54	-	60	130	-	144	59	-	65	140	-	159	64	-	72
5	7	170	123	-	136	56	-	62	133	-	147	60	-	67	143	-	163	65	-	74
5	8	173	126	-	139	57	-	63	136	-	150	62	-	68	146	-	167	66	-	76
5	9	175	129	-	142	59	-	64	139	-	153	63	-	69	149	-	170	68	-	77
5	10	178	132	-	145	60	-	66	142	-	156	64	-	71	152	-	173	69	-	78
5	11	180	135	-	148	61	-	67	145	-	159	66	-	72	155	-	176	70	-	80
6	0	183	138	-	151	63	-	68	148	-	162	67	-	73	158	-	179	72	-	81

thefreewindows.com

Male Chart for Normal Weight

Height			Small Frame					Medium Frame					Large Frame				
(ft)	(in)	(cm)	(lbs)		(lbs)	(kg)		(kg)	(lbs)		(lbs)	(kg)		(kg)	(lbs)		(lbs)	(kg)		(kg)
5	2	158	128	-	134	58	-	61	131	-	141	59	-	64	138	-	150	63	-	68
5	3	160	130	-	136	59	-	62	133	-	143	60	-	65	140	-	153	64	-	69
5	4	163	132	-	138	60	-	63	135	-	145	61	-	66	142	-	156	64	-	71
5	5	165	134	-	140	61	-	64	137	-	148	62	-	67	144	-	160	65	-	73
5	6	168	136	-	142	62	-	64	139	-	151	63	-	68	146	-	164	66	-	74
5	7	170	138	-	145	63	-	66	142	-	154	64	-	70	149	-	168	68	-	76
5	8	173	140	-	148	64	-	67	145	-	157	66	-	71	152	-	172	69	-	78
5	9	175	142	-	151	64	-	68	148	-	160	67	-	73	155	-	176	70	-	80
5	10	178	144	-	154	65	-	70	151	-	163	68	-	74	158	-	180	72	-	82
5	11	180	146	-	157	66	-	71	154	-	166	70	-	75	161	-	184	73	-	83
6	0	183	149	-	160	68	-	73	157	-	170	71	-	77	164	-	188	74	-	85
6	1	186	152	-	164	69	-	74	160	-	174	73	-	79	168	-	192	76	-	87
6	2	188	155	-	168	70	-	76	164	-	178	74	-	81	172	-	197	78	-	89
6	3	191	158	-	172	72	-	78	167	-	182	76	-	83	176	-	202	80	-	92
6	4	193	162	-	176	73	-	80	171	-	187	78	-	85	181	-	207	82	-	94

thefreewindows.com